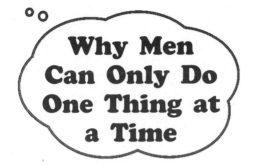

Why Men Can Only Do One Thing at a Time

Allan + Barbara Pease

and Women Never Stop Talking

Why Men Can Only Do One Thing at a Time ...

... and Women Never Stop Talking

Allan + Barbara Pease

ORION

Copyright © Allan and Barbara Pease 2003

First published in 1999 by Pease Training
International Pty Ltd

20 19 18 17 16 15 14 13

This revised combined edition published in 2003
by Orion Books Ltd

Orion House,
5 Upper St Martin's Lane,
London WC2H 9EA

An Hachette Livre UK Company

PUBLISHED BY ARRANGEMENT WITH
PEASE INTERNATIONAL PTY LTD

A CIP catalogue record for this book is
available from the British Library

Edited and designed by Jackie Freshfield

ISBN 978-0-7528-5629-4

Printed in Great Britain by Clays Ltd, St Ives plc

The Orion Publishing Group's policy is to use papers that
are natural, renewable and recyclable products and
made from wood grown in sustainable forests. The logging
and manufacturing processes are expected to conform to
the environmental regulations of the country of origin.

www.orionbooks.co.uk

Contents

Introduction

Men and women are different. Not better or worse – just different. About the only thing they have in common is that they belong to the same species. They live in different worlds, with different values and according to quite different sets of rules. Everyone knows this, but very few people, particularly men, are willing to admit it. Look at the evidence. Around 50% of marriages end in divorce in Western countries and most serious relationships stop short of becoming long-term. Men and women of every culture, creed and hue constantly argue over their partners' opinions, behaviour, attitudes and beliefs.

When a man goes to a toilet, he usually goes for one reason and one reason only. Women use toilets as social lounges and therapy rooms. Women who go to a toilet as strangers can come out best friends. But everyone would be instantly suspicious of the man who called out, 'Hey Frank, I'm going to the toilet. You wanna come with me?'

Men dominate TV remote controls and flick through the channels; women don't mind watching the commercials. Under pressure, men drink alcohol and invade other countries; women eat chocolate and go shopping.

Women criticise men for being insensitive, uncaring, not listening, not talking, not giving enough love, not being committed to relationships, wanting to have sex rather than make love and leaving the toilet seat up.

Men criticise women about their driving, for turning maps upside down, for their lack of a sense of direction, for talking too much, for not initiating sex often enough and for leaving the toilet seat down. Men can never find a pair of socks but their CDs are in alphabetical order. Women can always find the missing set of car keys, but rarely the most direct route to their destination. Men think they're the most sensible sex. Women *know* they are.

> *How many men does it take to*
> *change a roll of toilet paper?*
> *It's unknown. It's never happened.*

Women can't believe men are so unobservant. Men are amazed how a woman can't see a red flashing oil light on the car dashboard but can spot a dirty sock in a dark corner 50 metres away. Women are bewildered by men who can consistently parallel park a car in a tight spot using a rear-view mirror, but can never find the G-spot.

Society today is determined to believe that men and women possess exactly the same skills, aptitudes and potentials – just as science, ironically, is beginning to prove they are completely different.

And where does this leave us? As a society, on extremely shaky ground. It's only by understanding the differences between men and women that we can really start building on our collective strengths – rather than on our individual weaknesses. Enormous advances have been made in human evolutionary science and in this book we show how the lessons learned – when applied to male and female relationships – can give us all a solid and thorough understanding of the many strange things that happen between men and women ...

This book is dedicated to all the men and women who have ever sat up at 2.00am pulling their hair out as they plead with their partners, 'But *why* don't you understand?' Relationships fail because men still don't understand why a woman can't be more like a man, and women expect their men to behave just like they do. Not only will this book help you come to grips with the opposite sex, it'll help you understand yourself. And how you can both lead happier, healthier and more harmonious lives as a result, leading to relationships that can be fulfilling, enjoyable and satisfying.

... & Women Never Stop Talking

Same species ... different world

In the beginning...

Women gathered. Women nurtured.

Things were simple: he was the lunch-chaser, she was the nest-defender. The woman's role was clear. Being the child-bearer, her skills became specialised to meet that role. She needed to be able to monitor her surroundings for signs of danger, have excellent short-range navigational skills using land-marks to find her way, and have a highly-tuned ability to sense small changes in the behaviour and appearance of children and adults.

   Her success was measured by her ability to sustain family life. Her self-worth came from the man's appreciation of her home-making and nurturing skills. She was never expected to hunt animals, fight enemies or change light bulbs.

Men hunted. Men protected.

Man's job description was straightforward: he was a lunch-chaser, and that's all anyone expected of him. He would venture out each day into a hostile and dangerous world to risk his life as a hunter to bring food back to his woman and their children and he would defend them against savage animals or enemies. He developed long-distance navigational skills so he could locate food and bring it home, and excellent marksmanship skills so that he could hit a moving target.

His success as a man was measured by his ability to make a kill and bring it home, and his self-worth was measured by her appreciation for his struggle and effort.

There was never any need for him to 'analyse the relationship' and he wasn't expected to put out the garbage or help change the nappies.

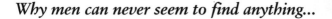

Why men can never seem to find anything...

...or so they say

Women are naturally intuitive

Women are equipped with far more finely-tuned sensory skills than men. As child-bearers and nest-defenders, they needed the ability to sense subtle mood and attitude changes in others that could signal pain, hunger, injury, aggression or depression. This is commonly called 'women's intuition'.

Women's intuition is something that has always bewildered men who play around – and are invariably caught.

'My wife can see a blonde hair on my coat from twenty feet, but she hits the garage door when she parks the car.'

A man would have to witness tears, a temper tantrum or be slapped around the face before he'd have a clue anything was going on

Males, being lunch-chasers, were never around the cave long enough to learn to read non-verbal signals or the ways of interpersonal communication.

Brain scan tests show that when a man's brain is in a resting state, at least 70% of its electrical activity is shut down. Scans of women's brains show a level 90% activity during the same state, confirming that women are constantly receiving and analysing information from their environment. A woman knows her children's friends, hopes, dreams, romances, secret fears, what they are thinking, how they are feeling and, usually, what mischief they are plotting. Men are vaguely aware of some short people also living in the house.

Women rarely get caught ogling other men due to their superior peripheral vision

Sex researchers report that women look at men's bodies as much as, and usually more than men look at women's. Women have a greater variety of cones in the retina of the eye – allowing them to describe colours in greater detail – and also have wider peripheral vision than men. As a nest-defender, a woman has brain software that allows her to receive an arc of at least 45° clear vision to each side of her head and above and below her nose. Some women's peripheral vision is effective up to almost 180°.

Men literally have 'tunnel vision'. That's why they're always so obvious when they look at other women. They have to turn their heads

A man's eyes are larger than a woman's and his brain configures them for a type of long-distance tunnel vision which means that he can see clearly and accurately directly in front of him, though over a much narrower field and over greater distances, almost like a pair of binoculars.

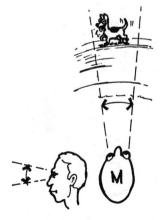

... & Women Never Stop Talking

Women always hide things from men

Well – actually they don't; it just feels like that to men. Men often accuse women of hiding things from them in drawers and cupboards. Socks, underwear, butter, car keys, wallets – they're all there, they just can't see them. With her wider arc of peripheral vision a woman can see most of the contents of a fridge or cupboard without moving her head. Her oestrogen hormones allow her to identify matching items in a drawer, cupboard or across a room and later remember objects in a complex random pattern – such as where the butter or jam is in the refrigerator.

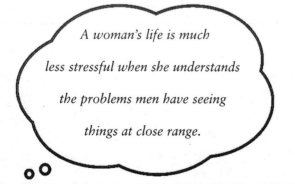

A woman's life is much less stressful when she understands the problems men have seeing things at close range.

Why Men Can Only Do One Thing at a Time...

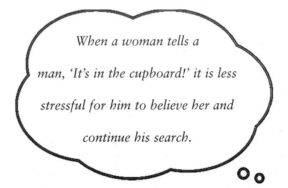

Modern man can find his way effortlessly to a distant pub, but can never find things in fridges and cupboards

New research suggests that male brains are searching in the fridge for the word B-U-T-T-E-R. If it's facing the wrong way, he virtually can't see it. Because of their tunnel vision, men move their heads from side to side and up and down as they scan for the 'missing' objects. Men's eyesight is configured for long distances: that's why they have difficulty locating things at close range – keys, socks, etc.

> *When a woman tells a man, 'It's in the cupboard!' it is less stressful for him to believe her and continue his search.*

... & Women Never Stop Talking

Women can fib better

Research reveals that, in face-to-face communications, non-verbal signals account for 60–80% of the impact of the message, while vocal sounds and words account for the balance. A woman's superior sensory equipment picks up and analyses this information and her brain's ability to rapidly transfer between hemispheres makes her more proficient at integrating and deciphering verbal, visual and other signals.

In other words, she can spot a fibber a mile off.

This is why most men have difficulty lying to a woman face-to-face.

Men can't fib their way out of a paper-bag

As most women know, lying to a man face-to-face is comparatively easy, as he does not have the necessary sensitivity to spot incongruities between her verbal and non-verbal signals.

Most men, if they're going to lie to a woman, would be far better off doing it over the phone, in a letter or with all the lights off, and a blanket over their head.

Woman: the walking lie detector

... & Women Never Stop Talking

Women can detect emotions through tone of voice

Women are more sensitive to differentiating tone changes, voice volume and pitch. This enables them to hear emotional changes in children and adults. This ability goes a long way to explaining the women's phrase, 'Don't use that tone of voice with me!' when arguing with men and boys. Most males don't have a clue what she's talking about.

> *Female hearing advantage contributes significantly to what is called 'Women's Intuition' and is one of the reasons why a woman can read between the lines of what people say.*

Men, er, can't

Men, however, shouldn't despair. They are excellent at identifying and imitating animal sounds, which would have been a significant advantage for the ancient hunter.

Sadly, there's not much call for this skill these days.

Boys are often chastised by 'grown-ups' for not listening. But as boys grow, particularly at puberty, their ear canals undergo growth spurts that can cause temporary deafness. Boys are equipped for more effective seeing than hearing. Female teachers have been found to reprimand girls differently to boys and seem intuitively to understand male and female hearing differences.

Female teachers continue to reprimand girls even if eye contact is lost. If a boy refuses eye contact, many female teachers intuitively understand that he probably either can't hear or is not listening, and will say, 'Look at me when I speak to you.'

In a room of fifty couples it takes the average woman less than ten minutes to have analysed the relationship between each couple in the room. She can see who's who, what's what and how they're all feeling.

Why Men Can Only Do One Thing at a Time...

It's not that men are insensitive to the small details.

Their brains just aren't organized to pick up the non-verbal signals that allow women to notice small details and changes in the appearance of others.

Men don't see the details

Lyn and Chris are driving home from a party. He's driving, she's navigating and they've just had an argument about her telling him to turn left when she really meant right. Nine minutes of silence has passed and he suspects something is up. 'Darling ... is everything OK?' asks Chris. 'Yes – everything's *fine!*' Lyn answers.

Her emphasis on the word 'fine' confirms that things are actually not fine. 'Did I do something wrong tonight?' asks Chris. 'I don't want to talk about it!' she snaps.

This means she's angry and *does* want to talk about it. Meanwhile, he's at a complete loss to understand what he's done to upset her. 'Please tell me. What did I do?' he pleads. 'I don't know what I did!'

In most conversations like this one, the man is telling the truth – he simply doesn't understand the problem. 'OK then,' she says, 'I'll tell you the problem even though you're playing that dumb act!' But it's not an act. He genuinely doesn't have a handle on the problem. She takes a deep breath. 'That bimbo was hanging around you all night giving you come-on signals – and you encouraged her!'

Now Chris is completely dumbstruck. What bimbo? What come-on signals? He didn't see anything. You see, while the 'bimbo' had been talking to him, he hadn't noticed that she was tilting her pelvis at him, flicking her hair, giving him longer than usual glances, stroking the stem of her wine glass and talking like a schoolgirl. He's a hunter. He doesn't have a woman's ability to pick up the visual, vocal and body language signals that say someone's on the make. Every woman at the party saw what the 'bimbo' was doing even without moving their heads. And a telepathic 'bitch alert' was sent and received by all other women at the party. Most of the men missed it completely.

So when a man claims he is telling the truth about these accusations, he probably is. Male brains are not equipped to hear or see details.

Men miss the details

It's a game of two minds...

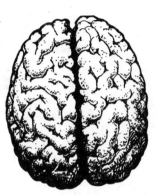

Left Hemisphere	Right Hemisphere
Right side of body	Left side of body
Mathematics	Creative
Verbal	Artistic
Logical	Visual
Facts	Intuition
Deduction	Ideas
Analysis	Imagination
Practical	Holistic
Order	Tune of a song
Words of a song	Sees 'big picture'
Lineal	Spatial
Sees fine details	Multiprocessing

Ask men and women if their brains work differently.
Men will say they think they do, in fact there was
something they were reading on the Internet the other
day ... Women will say, of course they do
– next question?

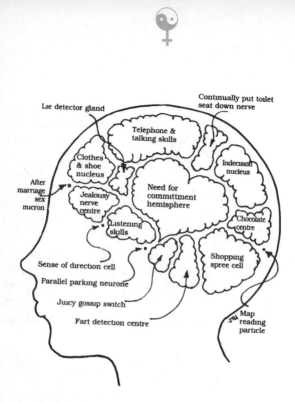

A woman's brain has a 10% thicker connnecting cord between the left and right lobes and up to 30% more connections. That's how she can walk, talk and apply lipstick – all at the same time.

Why Men Can Only Do One Thing at a Time...

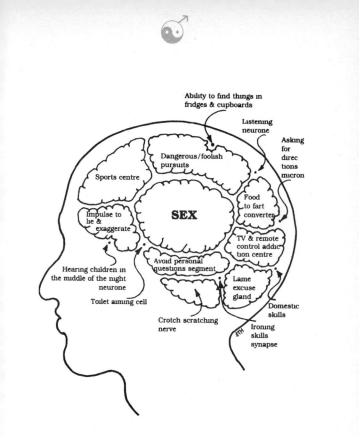

Men's brains are compartmentalised. That's why they can only concentrate on one thing at a time.

Women can multi-task with ease

A woman can do several unrelated things at the same time, and her brain is never disengaged. She can talk on a telephone at the same time as cooking a new recipe and watching television. Or she can drive a car, put on make-up and listen to the radio while talking on a hands-free telephone.

Because women use both sides of their brain, many find it more difficult to tell their left hand from their right. As a result, women all over the world are criticised by men for telling them to turn right – when they really meant left.

One thing at a time

If a man is cooking a recipe and you talk to him, he is likely to become angry because he can't follow the written instructions and listen at the same time.

If a man is shaving and you talk to him, he'll cut himself. If he's hammering and the doorbell rings, he'll hit his thumb. If you talk to him when he's driving, he'll miss the turn-off. These are excellent revenge tactics.

A man can either read or listen. He can't do both.

An archaeologist was digging through some rubble at an ancient site when he stumbled across a dusty old lamp. As he was rubbing off the dust, a genie popped out. 'You have freed me!' cried the genie. 'I will grant you a wish.'

The archaeologist thought for a moment, then replied, 'I wish for a bridge with a highway between England and France!'

The genie rolled his eyes and muttered, 'Hey, I just got out of this lamp and I'm cramped and tired. Do you have any idea how many miles it is between England and France? That's an engineering impossibility! Make another wish!'

The man pondered a little, then said, 'I wish I could understand how to communicate with women.'

The genie paled and asked, 'One lane or two?'

Talking and listening:

the art of communication

What females say   What males hear

'Once I didn't talk to my wife for

six months,' said the husband.

'I didn't want to interrupt!'

Every man's nightmare ...

Barbara and Allan were getting ready to go to a cocktail party. Barbara had bought a new dress and wanted to look her best. She held up two pairs of shoes, one blue, one gold. Then she asked Allan the question that all men fear, 'Darling, which should I wear with this dress?'

A cold chill ran down Allan's back. He knew he was in trouble. 'Ahh ... umm ... whichever you like sweetheart,' he stammered. 'Come on Allan,' she said, impatiently. 'Which looks better ... blue or gold?' 'Gold!' he replied, nervously. 'So, what's wrong with the blue?' she asked. 'You've never liked them! I paid a fortune for them and you hate them, don't you?'

Allan's shoulders slumped. 'If you don't want my opinion, Barbara, don't ask!' he said. He thought he'd been asked to fix a problem but, when he solved it, she wasn't at all grateful. Barbara, however, was using a typical female speech trait: indirect speech. She'd already decided which shoes she was going to wear and didn't want another opinion; she wanted confirmation that she looked good. In this section, we'll look at the problems men and women have communicating with each other and offer some novel solutions.

The 'blue or gold shoes' strategy

If a woman asks 'blue or gold?' when selecting shoes, it's important that a man does not give an answer. Instead, he should ask, 'Have you chosen a pair, darling?' Most women are taken aback by this approach because most men they know immediately state a preference. 'Well ... I thought I could possibly wear the gold ...' she'll say, uncertainly. The reality is, she has already chosen the gold shoes. 'Why the gold?' he'll ask. 'Because I'm wearing gold accessories and my dress has a gold pattern in it,' she'll respond. A skilled man would then reply, 'Great choice! You'll look fabulous! You've done well! I love it!' And you can bet he'll have a great night.

It's good to talk

Women are good conversationalists. They enjoy it, and do lots of it. With specific areas to control speech, the rest of a woman's brain is available for other tasks, enabling her to do a range of different things at once while talking.

This allows girls to learn foreign languages faster and easier than boys, and also explains why girls are better at grammar, punctuation and spelling. Girls have more legible writing too.

When reporting back after a party, a teenage girl will give a detailed report of everything – who said what to whom, how everyone felt and what they were wearing. A teenage boy when asked to comment on the same party would just mumble '... Uh ... good.'

Can't talk, won't talk

For males, speech and language are not critical brain skills. They operate mainly in the left brain and have less specific locations. When a male talks, MRI scans show that his left hemisphere becomes active as it searches to find a centre for speaking, but is unable to find much. Consequently, men aren't much good at talking.

Young boys don't do as well at school because their verbal abilities are inferior to those of girls. As a result, they perform poorly in languages, English and the arts. They feel stupid in front of the more articulate girls and become boisterous and disruptive.

On Valentine's Day, florists tell men to 'say it with flowers' because they know that a man finds it difficult to say it with words. Buying a card is never a problem for a man, it's what to write inside that stumps him.

Unpacking

At the end of a stressful day a man's mono-tracking brain can file all his problems away but the female brain does not store information in this way. Her worries just keep going around and around in her head.

The only way a woman gets rid of the problems from her mind is by talking about them to acknowledge them. Therefore, when a woman talks at the end of the day, her objective is to discharge the problems, not to find conclusions or solutions.

Cold storage

Male brains are highly compartmentalised and have the ability to separate and store information and problems.

A man can file away his problems. When a woman shares her problems at the end of the day, she doesn't want interruptions with solutions. You are not expected to respond, just to listen and offer support.

All talk

A woman talks to show participation and build relationships. If a woman is talking to you a lot, she likes you. If she's not talking to you, you're in trouble.

For a woman, speech has a clear purpose: to build relationships and make friends – not to solve problems. A woman can spend two weeks on vacation with her girlfriend and, when she returns home, telephone the same girlfriend and talk for another two hours.

All quiet on the western front

For men, not talking is perfectly natural.

For men, to talk is to relate the facts. Men see the telephone as a communication tool for relaying facts and information to other people, but a woman sees it as a means of bonding.

> All men hate to hear 'We need to talk about our relationship.' These seven words would strike fear even into the heart of Superman.

Giving 'the silent treatment'

If a woman wants to punish you she won't talk. Men call this 'the silent treatment'. The threat from a woman of, 'I'll never talk to you again!' is one to be taken seriously.

Taking 'the silent treatment'

When a man is being given 'the silent treatment', it will take him around nine minutes of silence to realise that he's being punished. Until the nine-minute mark is reached, he sees her silence as a kind of bonus – he's getting some 'peace and quiet'.

How women talk

With a greater flow of information between left and right hemispheres and specific brain locations for speech, most women can talk about several subjects simultaneously – sometimes in a single sentence. It's like juggling three or four balls at once and most women seem to do it effortlessly. Not only that, but women can juggle several subjects with other women who are all doing the same thing – and no-one ever seems to drop a ball.

This multi-tracking ability is frustrating for a man as the male brain is mono-tracked and can only handle one subject at a time. When women are multi-tracking, men can become completely dazed and confused.

How men talk

A man's sentences are shorter than a woman's and are more structured. They usually have a simple opening, a clear point and a conclusion. It's easy to follow what he means or wants. If you multi-track several subjects with a man, he gets lost. It's important for a woman to understand that if you want to be convincing or persuasive with a man, you should present only one clear thought or idea at a time.

Men were never great conversationalists

... & Women Never Stop Talking

Emote

In women, vocabulary is front and back of both hemi-spheres and is not a strong ability. Consequently, definition and the meaning of words is not important to a woman because she relies on voice intonation for meaning and body language for emotional content.

Define

Men use language to compete with women and other men and definition becomes an important tactic in playing the game. If one man is trying to make a strong or forceful point and says, for example, '... he wasn't making his point clearly or getting to the bottom line so that everyone could understand what he meant', another man may interrupt with, 'He didn't articulate?', to better define the point being made and 'get one up' on the first man.

Because vocabulary is not a hotspot in a woman's brain, she can feel that the precise definition of words is irrelevant. She'll then take poetic licence with words, or won't shy away from exaggeration simply for effect. Men, however, interpret every word she says as if it is true and respond accordingly.

In an argument, a man defines a woman's words to try to win. See if you recognise this exchange:

> *Robyn:* 'You *never* agree with anything I say.'
> *John:* 'What do you mean *never*? I agreed with your last two points didn't I?'
> *Robyn:* 'You *always* disagree with me and you *always* want to be right!'
> *John:* 'Not true! I don't *always* disagree with you! I agreed with you this morning, I agreed with you last night and I agreed with you last Saturday so you can't say I *always* disagree!'
> *Robyn:* 'You say this *every* time I bring it up!'
> *John:* 'That's a lie! I don't say it *every* time!'
> *Robyn:* 'And you *only* ever touch me when you want sex!'
> *John:* 'Stop exaggerating! I don't *only* ever ...'

Why Men Can Only Do One Thing at a Time...

She continues arguing, using emotions to fight him; he keeps defining her words. The argument escalates to the point where she refuses to talk or he stomps off to be on his own. But to argue successfully, a man needs to understand that a woman will use words that she doesn't really mean, so he shouldn't take them literally or define them. Take, for example, when a woman says, 'If I sat next to a woman who was wearing the identical dress, I'd just die! There's nothing worse!' She doesn't really mean that there is *nothing worse* or that she really expects to *die*, but a man's literal mind may respond with, 'No, you won't die, there are worse things than that!' which sounds sarcastic to a woman. By the same token, however, a woman needs to learn that she'll have to argue logically with a man if she wants to win and to only give him one thought at a time. And women should never multi-track in an argument – their barbs have no chance of hitting home.

How women listen

A woman reads the meaning of what is being said through voice intonation and the speaker's body language. Typically, a woman can use an average of six listening expressions in a ten-second period to reflect, and then feed back the speaker's emotions. Her face will mirror the emotions being expressed by the speaker. To someone watching, it can almost look as if the events being discussed are happening to both women.

Here is a typical ten-second sequence of a woman showing she is listening:

Sadness   Surprise   Anger   Joy   Fear   Desire

This is exactly what a man needs to do to capture a woman's attention and keep her listening. Most men are daunted by the prospect of using facial feedback while listening, but it pays big dividends for the man who becomes adept at the art.

How men listen

The biological objective of our male warrior when listening was to remain impassive, so as not to betray his emotions.

Here is the same range of facial expressions used by a man in a ten-second listening period

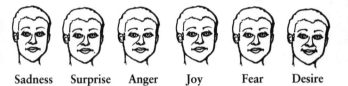

Sadness   Surprise   Anger   Joy   Fear   Desire

This emotionless mask that men use while listening allows them to feel in control of the situation, but does not mean a man does not experience emotions. Brain scans reveal that men feel emotion as strongly as women, but avoid showing it.

For a woman, having a sense of humour doesn't mean telling jokes.

It means you laugh at his jokes.

Spatial awareness:

the art of map-reading and

parallel parking

'Oh no! I can't believe this, girls … Look at this map!
… I think we were supposed to turn right at that big
green mountain …'

How a map almost led to divorce

Ray and Ruth were on their way to see a show in the city. Ray always drove. They never discussed why he always drove, he just did. And, like most men, he became a different person behind the wheel.

Ray asked Ruth to look up the address in the street directory. She opened it at the appropriate page and then turned the directory upside down. She rotated it to the right way up and then turned it upside down again. Then she sat silently and stared at it. She understood what a map meant but, when it came to applying it to where they were going, it seemed strangely irrelevant. It was like studying geography in school. All those pink and green shapes bore little resemblance to the real world in which she lived. Sometimes she coped with the map when they were heading North, but South was a disaster – and they were heading South. She rotated the map one more time. After several more seconds of silence, Ray spoke.

'Stop turning the map upside down!' he snapped.

'But I need to face it in the direction we're going,' Ruth explained, meekly.

'Yeah, but you can't read it upside down!' Ray barked.

'Look Ray, it makes logical sense to face the map in the direction we need to go. That way I can match the street signs with the directory!' she said, raising her voice indignantly.

'Yeah, but if the map was supposed to be read upside down, they'd print the writing upside down, right? Stop fooling around and tell me where to go!'

'I'll tell you where to go all right!' responded Ruth, furiously. She threw the street directory at him and shouted, 'Read it yourself!'

Does this argument sound familiar? It's one of the most common between men and women of all races, and it stretches back thousands of years. In the 11th century, Lady Godiva rode her horse naked down the wrong Coventry street, Juliet got lost trying to get back home after a love tryst with Romeo, Cleopatra threatened Marc Antony with castration for trying to force her to understand his battle maps and the Wicked Witch of the West often headed South, North or East.

Spatially challenged

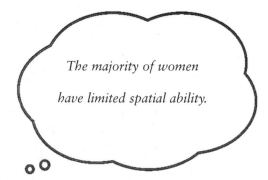

The majority of women have limited spatial ability.

Spatial ability means being able to picture in the mind the shape of things, their dimensions, co-ordinates, proportions, movement and geography. It also involves being able to imagine an object being rotated in space, navigating around an obstacle course and seeing things in three-dimensions.

Reading maps and understanding where you are relies on spatial ability. Spatial ability is located in both brain hemispheres for women but does not have measurable locations as it does in males. Only about 10% of women have spatial abilities that are as dynamic as those of the best men.

Girls are excellent at seeing two dimensions but seeing in three dimensions requires high spatial ability.

Spatial champion

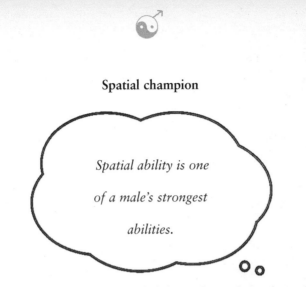

Spatial ability is one of a male's strongest abilities.

Brain scans show that spatial ability is located mostly in the right brain for men and boys. It developed from ancient times to allow men, the hunters, to calculate the speed, movement and distance of prey, work out how fast they had to run to catch their targets, and know how much force they needed to kill their lunch with a rock or a spear.

Boys are far more able to see a third dimension, giving depth.

Taking the long route home

Spatial ability is not strong in women and girls because being able to chase animals and find the way home was never part of woman's job description. This is why many women have trouble reading a map or street directory.

Most women don't enjoy spatial activities and don't pursue careers or pastimes that require them.

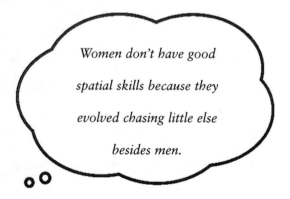

Women don't have good spatial skills because they evolved chasing little else besides men.

Why Men Can Only Do One Thing at a Time...

Right on target

Modern man no longer has to catch lunch. Today, he uses his spatial ability for playing golf, computer games, football and any sport or activity involving chasing something or aiming at a target.

When the requirements for the job is pure spatial ability and mathematical reasoning, men still dominate. This is why 91% of all engineers and 98% of cockpit crews are male.

Lost

Around 90% of women have limited spatial ability compared to the average man. That's why they have so much trouble programming a video recorder.

Go to any city in the world and watch female tourists standing at junctions furiously turning their maps around and looking lost. Visit a multi-storey car park at any shopping mall and watch female shoppers gloomily wandering around trying to find their cars.

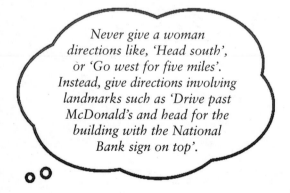

Never give a woman directions like, 'Head south', or 'Go west for five miles'. Instead, give directions involving landmarks such as 'Drive past McDonald's and head for the building with the National Bank sign on top'.

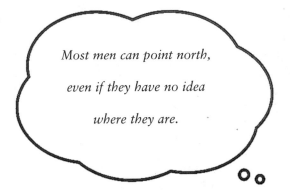

Found

Spatial ability allows a man to rotate a map in his mind and know in which direction to go. If he has to return to the same location at a later time, he doesn't need the map, as his spatial area can store the information. Most males can read a map while facing North and know that they need to go South. Most men, if put in an unfamiliar room with no windows, can point North. As a lunch-chaser, he needed to find his way back home or there would be little chance of survival.

Most men can point north,

even if they have no idea

where they are.

How to avoid an argument

Men love to drive fast around winding roads because their spatial skills come into play – gear ratios, clutch and brake combinations, relative speed to corners, angles and distances. And they do it with the radio turned off.

The modern male driver sits behind the wheel, hands his wife a map and asks her to navigate. With limited spatial ability she becomes silent, starts turning the map around and feels incompetent. Then she tries to identify something on the horizon that resembles something on the map. Most men don't understand that if you don't have specific areas in the brain for mental map rotation, you'll rotate it in your hands. It makes perfect sense to a woman to face a map in the direction she is travelling.

Having spatial ability on both sides of the brain interferes with a female's speech function, so if you give a woman a street directory, she'll stop talking before she turns it around. Give it to a man and he'll continue talking – but he'll also turn the radio off because he can't operate his hearing functions at the same time as his map-reading skills. That's why when a phone rings in his home he demands that everyone keeps quiet while he answers it.

Thoughts, attitudes, emotions

and other disaster areas

Colin and Jill were driving to a party in an unfamiliar area. It should have taken them 20 minutes. It had already taken them 50, and there was still no sign of their destination. Colin was becoming grumpy and Jill started feeling despondent as they passed the same garage for the third time.

> *Jill:* 'Darling, I think we should have turned right at the garage. Let's stop and ask directions.'
>
> *Colin:* 'There's no problem. I know it's around here somewhere ...'
>
> *Jill:* 'But we're half-an-hour late already and the party's started – let's stop and ask someone!'
>
> *Colin:* 'Listen, I know what I'm doing! Do you want to drive or are you going to let me?'
>
> *Jill:* 'No, I don't want to drive, but I don't want to drive in circles all night either!'
>
> *Colin:* 'OK then, why don't I just turn the car around and we'll go back home!'

Most men and women will recognise this conversation. A woman can't understand why this wonderful man she loves so much suddenly turns into Mad Max on steroids just because he's lost. If she was lost, she'd ask for directions, so what's his problem? Why can't he admit he doesn't know?

Why Men Can Only Do One Thing at a Time...

Why did Moses spend 40 years

wandering in the desert?

He refused to ask for directions.

Women don't mind admitting mistakes because, in their world, it's seen as a form of bonding and building trust. The last man to admit he'd made a mistake, however, was General Custer.

Men and women perceive the same world through different eyes. A man sees things and objects and their relationship to each other in a spatial way, as though he was putting the pieces of a jigsaw puzzle together. Women literally take in a bigger, wider picture and see the fine detail, but the individual pieces of the puzzles and their relationship to the next piece is more relevant than their spatial positioning.

Male awareness is concerned with getting results, achieving goals, status and power and beating the competition. Female awareness is focused on communication, co-operation, harmony, love, sharing and our relationship to one another. This contrast is so great that it's amazing men and women can even consider living together in the first place.

Girl talk

Girls talk about who likes who or who is angry with who. They play in small groups and share 'secrets' about others as a form of bonding. As teenagers, girls talk about boys, weight, clothes and their friends. As adults, women talk about diet, personal relationships, marriage, children, lovers, personalities, clothes, the actions of others, work relationships and anything to do with people and personal issues.

Women rarely withhold when it comes to sex talk. They freely discuss techniques, strategies, times and sizes. And they are graphic in their descriptions.

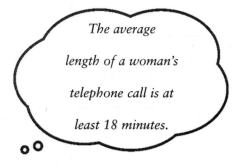

The average length of a woman's telephone call is at least 18 minutes.

Boy talk

Boys talk about things and activities – who did what, who is good at something and how things work. As teenagers, they talk about sports, the mechanics and function of things. As men they discuss sports, their work, news, what they did or where they went, technology, cars and mechanical gadgets.

Men rarely discuss the intimate details of sex in case they don't match up to their mates' vital statistics.

> *The average length of a man's telephone call is less than 3 minutes.*

WOMEN'S ENGLISH

Yes = No.

No = Yes.

Maybe = No.

I'm sorry = You'll be sorry.

We need = I want.

It's your decision = The correct decision should be obvious by now.

Do what you want = You'll pay for this later.

We need to talk = I need to complain.

Sure ... go ahead = I don't want you to.

I'm not upset = Of course I'm upset, you moron!

You're ... so manly = You need a shave and you sweat a lot.

You're certainly attentive tonight = Is sex all you ever think about?

Be romantic, turn out the lights = I have flabby thighs.

This kitchen is so inconvenient = I want a new house.

I want new curtains = and carpeting, and furniture, and wallpaper...

Hang the picture there = NO, I mean hang it there!

Do you love me? = I'm going to ask for something expensive.

How much do you love me? = I did something today you're really not going to like.

I'll be ready in a minute = Kick off your shoes and find a good game on TV.

Is my bum fat? = Tell me I'm beautiful.

You have to learn to communicate = Just agree with me.

Are you listening to me!? = [Too late, you're dead.]

Was that the baby? = Why don't you get out of bed and walk him until he goes to sleep.

I'm not yelling! = Yes I am yelling because I think this is important.

Why Men Can Only Do One Thing at a Time...

MEN'S ENGLISH

I'm hungry = I'm hungry.
I'm sleepy = I'm sleepy.
I'm tired = I'm tired.
Do you want to go to a film? = I'd eventually like to have sex with you.
Can I take you out to dinner? = I'd eventually like to
have sex with you.
Can I call you sometime? = I'd eventually like to have sex with you.
May I have this dance? = I'd eventually like to have sex with you.
Nice dress! = Nice cleavage!
You look tense, let me give you a massage = I want to fondle you.
What's wrong? = What meaningless, self-inflicted psychological
trauma are you going through now?
What's wrong? = I guess sex tonight is out of the question.
I'm bored = Do you want to have sex?
I love you = Let's have sex now.
I love you, too = OK, I said it ....We'd better have sex now!
Yes, I like the way you cut your hair = I liked it better before.
Yes, I like the way you cut your hair = £50 and it doesn't look that
much different!
Let's talk = I am trying to impress you by showing that I am a deep
person and maybe then you'd like to have sex with me.
Will you marry me? = I want to make it illegal for you to have sex
with other guys.

... & Women Never Stop Talking

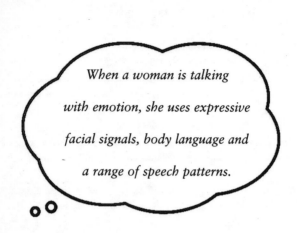

When a woman is talking with emotion, she uses expressive facial signals, body language and a range of speech patterns.

Why Men Can Only Do One Thing at a Time...

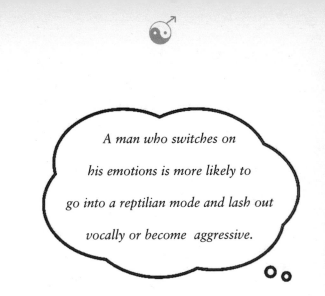

A man who switches on
his emotions is more likely to
go into a reptilian mode and lash out
vocally or become aggressive.

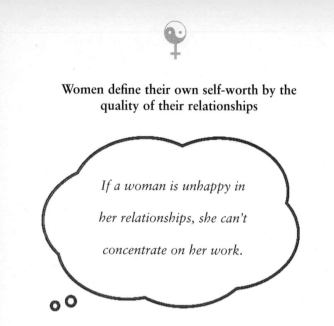

Women define their own self-worth by the quality of their relationships

If a woman is unhappy in her relationships, she can't concentrate on her work.

Under stress or pressure, a woman sees spending time talking with her man as a reward, but a man sees it as an interference in his problem-solving process. She wants to talk and cuddle, and he wants to watch the football. To a woman, he seems uncaring and disinterested and a man sees her as annoying or pedantic. These perceptions are the reflections of the different organisation and priorities of their brains. This is why a woman always says that the relationship seems more important to her than it does to him – it is. Understanding this difference will take the pressure off you and your partner, and you will not judge each other's behaviour so harshly.

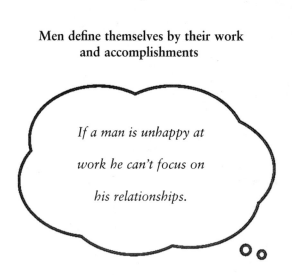

Men define themselves by their work and accomplishments

If a man is unhappy at work he can't focus on his relationships.

A man's brain is organised for a 'how-do-I-fix-it?' response to life. Men use this 'fix it' criterion in their approach to almost everything they do. One woman told us that she wanted her husband to show a more loving attitude towards her – so he mowed the lawn. He saw this as an expression of his love. When she said she still wasn't happy, he painted the kitchen. And when this didn't work, he offered to take her to the football. When a woman is upset she will talk emotionally to her friends, but an upset man will rebuild a motor or fix a leaking tap.

Women admit mistakes

A man won't admit mistakes because he thinks she won't love him. But the reality is, a woman loves a man more when he will admit mistakes.

A woman needs to make sure that she doesn't make a man feel wrong when she discusses problems with him. Even giving a man a self-help book for his birthday is often interpreted by him as, 'You're not good enough.'

Men hate criticism – that's why
they like to marry virgins.

A man needs to understand that a woman's objective is not to make him wrong; it's to help him and he should not take things personally.

If a man says something in the woods and no woman hears him, is he still wrong?

Men are never wrong?

A million years of not wanting to be seen as a failure seems to be wired into modern man's brain. If a man is driving in the car alone, he'd probably stop and ask directions. But to do it when a woman is in the car makes him feel a failure.

When a woman says, 'Let's ask directions', a man hears: 'You're incompetent, you can't navigate'. If she says, 'The kitchen tap is leaking, let's call a plumber', he hears, 'You're useless, I'll get another man to do it!' This is also the reason men have difficulty saying, 'I'm sorry'. They see it as admitting they are wrong, and to be wrong is to fail.

A Sunday drive

... & Women Never Stop Talking

Stress

Uptight men drink alcohol and invade

other countries.

Uptight women eat chocolate and invade

shopping centres.

Under pressure, women talk without thinking and men act without thinking. That's why 90% of people in jails are men and 90% of people who see therapists are women. When men and women are both under pressure it can be an emotional minefield as each tries to cope. Men stop talking and women become worried about it. Women start talking and men can't handle it. To help him feel better she tries to encourage him to talk about the problem, which is the worst thing she can do. He tells her to leave him alone and retreats to another location.

Because she's also under pressure, she wants to talk about her problems, which frustrates him even more. When he retreats to his problem-solving mode she feels rejected and unloved and calls her mother, sister or friends.

The Complete Shut Off

One of the least understood stress differences between men and women is the complete shut out. A man will completely shut everyone out when he is under extreme stress or needs to find a solution to a serious problem. A man totally disconnects the part of his brain that controls emotion, goes into problem-solving mode and stops talking. When a man uses the complete shut-out, it can be terrifying for a woman because she only does this when she has been hurt, lied to or abused. A woman assumes that this must also be the case with a man – she must have hurt him and he doesn't love her anymore. She tries to encourage him to talk but he refuses, thinking she doesn't have faith in his ability to solve his problems. When a woman feels hurt, she shuts off and a man thinks she needs space and so he goes to the pub with his friends or cleans the carburettor in his car. If a man completely shuts off, let him do it, he'll be fine. If a woman shuts off, there's trouble brewing and it's time for deep discussion.

Share the remote control with the woman in your life

A man flicking the channels with the remote control is one of women's pet hates.

Women don't flick channels – they watch a programme and search for the storyline, the feelings and relationships of those involved in the story. Newspaper addiction serves the same purpose for men. Women need to understand that when men do these things they can't hear or remember much, so it is difficult to try to talk with them.

**In a man's heaven, he has three remote controls,
and the toilet seat is always left up**

A man loves to control the TV remote. He sits there like a zombie just channel-hopping, not paying attention to any particular programme. When a man does this, he is mentally problem solving and often doesn't even see what's happening on each station. He just searches for the bottom line in each story. By channel-flicking he can forget about his problems and look for solutions to other people's.

Women: Eating Out

Women see eating out as a way to build and nurture a relationship, discuss problems or support a friend.

When eating out, women call everyone by their first names because this builds relationships. If Barbara, Robyn, Lisa and Fiona go to lunch they will call each other Barbara, Robyn, Lisa and Fiona.

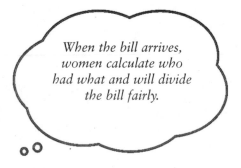

When the bill arrives, women calculate who had what and will divide the bill fairly.

Men: Eating Out

Men see eating out as a logical approach to food – no cooking, shopping or cleaning up.

When out, men will avoid any intimacy with other men. If Ray, Allan, Mike and Bill go out for a drink, they refer to each other as Dickhead, Wanker, Numbskull and Useless. These names avoid any hint of intimacy.

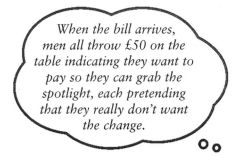

When the bill arrives, men all throw £50 on the table indicating they want to pay so they can grab the spotlight, each pretending that they really don't want the change.

How to Shower Like a Woman

Take off clothing and place it in laundry hampers according to lights, darks, whites, man-made or natural.

Walk to bathroom wearing long dressing gown. If husband seen along the way cover up any exposed flesh and rush to the bathroom.

Look at womanly physique in the mirror and stick out belly. Complain and whine about getting fat.

Get in shower. Look for facecloth, arm cloth, loin cloth, long loofah, wide loofah and pumice stone.

Wash hair twice with cucumber and grapefruit shampoo with 83 added vitamins.

Condition hair with cucumber and grapefruit conditioner with enhanced natural crocus oil. Leave on hair for 15 minutes.

Wash face with crushed apricot scrub for ten minutes until red raw.

Wash entire rest of body with Ginger Nut and Jaffa Cake body wash.

Rinse conditioner off hair taking at least 15 minutes to make sure that it's all come off.

Shave armpits and legs. Consider shaving bikini area but decide to get it waxed instead.

Scream loudly when husband flushes toilet and water loses pressure and turns red hot.

Turn off shower. Wipe all surfaces in shower. Spray mould spots with Tilex.

Get out of shower. Dry with towel the size of small African country.

Wrap hair in super-absorbent second towel.

Check entire body for remotest sign of spots.

Return to bedroom wearing long dressing gown and towel on head.

If husband seen, cover up any exposed areas and then rush to bedroom to spend an hour and a half getting dressed.

Why Men Can Only Do One Thing at a Time...

How to Shower Like a Man

Take off clothes while sitting on bed and leave them in a pile.
Walk naked to bathroom.
If wife seen, shake wedding tackle at her while shouting "Woo, Woo!"
Look in mirror and suck in gut to see your manly physique. Admire size of penis in mirror, scratch balls and smell fingers.
Get in shower.
Don't bother to look for wash cloth, don't need one.
Wash face.
Wash armpits.
Laugh at how loud farts sound in the shower.
Wash balls and the surrounding area.
Wash arse, leaving hair on soap.
Shampoo hair but do not use conditioner.
Make Mohican hairstyle with shampoo. Pull back curtain to see self in mirror.
Pee in shower, aiming for the centre hole.
Rinse off and get out of shower. Fail to notice water on floor because shower curtain outside bath for whole shower time.
Partially dry off.
Look at self in mirror, flex muscles and admire size of wedding tackle again.
Leave shower curtain open and wet bath mat on floor.
Leave bathroom light and fan on.
Return to bedroom with towel around waist. If you pass wife, pull off towel, grab wedding tackle, go "Yeah baby" and thrust pelvis at her.
Fart twice.
Put on yesterday's clothes.

... & Women Never Stop Talking

THINGY (thing-ee) n. For a **female**: Any part under a car's bonnet. For a **male**: The strap fastener on a woman's bra.

VULNERABLE (vul-ne-ra-bel) adj. **Female**: Fully opening up one's self emotionally to another. **Male**: Playing cricket without a helmet, box or pads.

COMMUNICATION (ko-myoo-ni-kay-shon) n. **Female**: The open sharing of thoughts and feelings with one's partner. **Male**: Scratching out a note before suddenly taking off for a weekend with the boys.

COMMITMENT (ko-mit-ment) n. **Female**: A desire to get married and raise a family. **Male**: Not trying to pick up other women while out with one's girlfriend.

ENTERTAINMENT (en-ter-tayn-ment) n. **Female**: A good movie, concert, play or book. **Male**: Anything that can be done while drinking.

FLATULENCE (flach-u-lents) n. **Female**: An embarrassing by-product of digestion. **Male**: An endless source of entertainment, self-expression and male bonding.

MAKING LOVE (may-king luv) n. **Female**: The greatest expression of intimacy a couple can achieve. **Male**: What a woman does while a man is bonking her.

REMOTE CONTROL (ri-moht kon-trohl) n. **Female**: A device for changing from one TV channel to another. **Male**: A device for scanning through all 54 channels every three minutes.

Men, *women and sex*

Q: What's the difference between PMT and BSE?

**A: One is Mad Cow Disease.
The other is an agricultural problem.**

Between 21–28 days after menstruation, female hormones dramatically drop, creating severe withdrawal symptoms known as PMT. For many women, this causes feelings of doom, gloom, depression, and even suicidal tendencies. One woman in 25 suffers so severely from their hormones being out of balance, she can undergo personality changes.

Never raise your hand to a woman with PMT. It leaves your groin unprotected.

'Let me get this straight, Mrs Goodwin. You say you're suffering PMT, you warned your husband that unless he stopped flicking channels on the remote control you'd blow his brains out ... How did he respond?'

Why Men Can Only Do One Thing at a Time...

Hormone overdrive

Testosterone is the hormone of success, achievement and competitiveness and in the wrong hands (or testicles) makes men and male animals potentially dangerous. Most parents are aware of the almost insatiable desire that young boys have to watch violent movies and how their sons can accurately recall and describe aggressive scenes in detail. Girls are generally uninterested in these types of movies.

Creatures with the highest testosterone
levels rule the animal kingdom

Ninety-two per cent of horn tooting at traffic lights is done by men, while they also carry out 96% of burglaries and 88% of murders. Practically all sexual deviants are male, and tests on deviant women show high male hormone levels.

Why does a man's penis have a hole in it?

So he can get oxygen to his brain.

Female sex drive

Women's sex drive is like an electric oven – it heats slowly to its top temperature and takes a lot longer to cool down.

The average woman's sex drive gradually increases so that her sexual peak is between the ages of 36–38, which explains the 'toy boy' syndrome of the older woman/younger man. A man's sexual performance level at age 19 is more compatible with a woman in her late 30s to early 40s.

Male sex drive

Male sex drive is like a microwave – it operates at full capacity within seconds, and can be turned off just as quickly when the meal is cooked.

A man's testosterone level slowly decreases as he gets older and his sex drive decreases accordingly. The sex drive of a man in his 40s is compatible with a woman in her early 20s which partly explains the older man/younger woman combination. There is usually a 10 to 20-year age difference between these older/younger combinations.

Male menopause is a lot more fun than female menopause. With female menopause you gain weight and get hot flushes. Male menopause – you get to date young girls and ride motorcycles.

No sex, please, we're female.

A woman's sex drive is significantly affected by events in her life. If she hates her job, she has a really demanding project at work, the mortgage repayments have just doubled, the kids are sick, she was drenched in the rain or the dog ran away, sex will not even be a consideration. All she can think about is going to bed and sleeping.

Sex. Now. Please.

When the same events happen to a man, he sees sex as a sleeping pill – a way of releasing the built-up tensions of the day. So, at the end of the day, he puts the hard word on the woman, she calls him an insensitive moron, he calls her frigid and he gets to sleep on the couch.

Men don't mind sleeping on the couch.

It's like camping.

A woman wants lots of sex with the man she loves

There's a small percentage of women who are as promiscuous as men, but their motivation differs from men. To be turned on sexually, nest-defending human female's brain circuitry responds to a range of criteria other than just the promise of sex. Most women want a relationship or at least some emotional connection before they feel the desire for sex.

Most men don't realise that once a woman feels an emotional bond has been created, she will happily bonk his brains out for the next three to six months.

A man just wants lots of sex

Promiscuity is wired into a man's brain. He has enormous amounts of testosterone to fulfil his ancient urge to procreate so he is not biologically inclined to monogamy. Some men think that monogamy is what furniture is made out of.

If unrestrained, most men would fall into a bottomless pit of mindless fornication to guarantee survival of the tribe.

A man decided to march in the holy crusades. Concluding that his wife should wear a chastity belt while he is gone, he locks up her nether regions and gives the key to his best friend.

He tells him, 'If I do not return within four years, unlock my wife and set her free to live a normal life.'

So, the husband leaves on horseback and about a half hour later, he sees a cloud of dust behind him. He waits for it to come closer and sees his best friend.

'What's wrong?' he asks.

'You gave me the wrong key!'

... & Women Never Stop Talking

Most women prefer sex with the lights out – they can't bear to see a man enjoying himself.

Why Men Can Only Do One Thing at a Time...

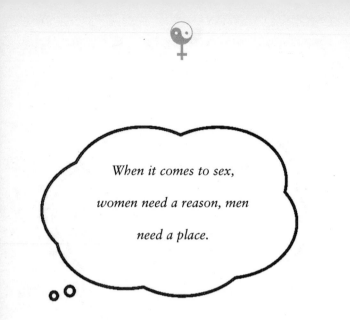

When it comes to sex,

women need a reason, men

need a place.

A woman doesn't want sex for the same reasons a man does. A woman enters a new relationship looking for romance and love. Sex comes as a consequence.

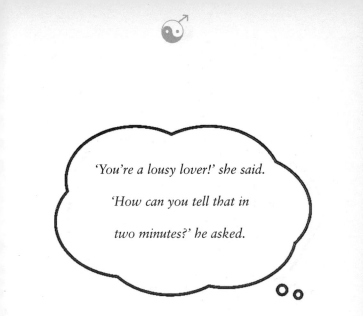

'You're a lousy lover!' she said.

'How can you tell that in

two minutes?' he asked.

From a cold start to orgasm, a healthy man's average time is around two-and-a-half minutes. For a healthy woman, the same average is 13 minutes. For most mammals, copulation is a fast affair because with their minds on other things, they become vulnerable to attack. The 'quickie' was Nature's way of preserving the species.

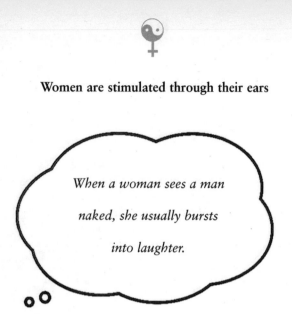

Women are stimulated through their ears

When a woman sees a man naked, she usually bursts into laughter.

Women, with their greater range of sensory information receptors, want to hear sweet words rather than look at the male shape. A woman's sensitivity to hearing wonderful compliments is so strong, many women even close their eyes when their lover whispers sweet nothings.

Men are stimulated through their eyes

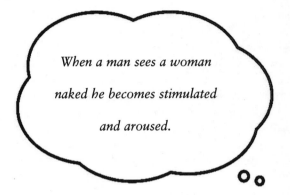

When a man sees a woman naked he becomes stimulated and aroused.

Men's brains are wired to look at female shapes. This is why erotic images have so much impact on them.

Ogling: The Facts

When a woman with a nice body walks by, a man, lacking good peripheral vision, turns his head to look and goes into a trance-like state. His blinking ceases and saliva fills his mouth, a reaction described by women as 'drooling'. If a couple are walking down the street and Miss Mini Skirt comes swaying towards them on the other side of the street, the woman's wide-range peripheral vision allows her to spot the other woman before the man does. She'll make quick comparisons between herself and the potential competitor, usually negative ones against herself. When the man eventually spots her he receives a negative reaction from his woman for ogling. A woman will usually have two negative thoughts in this situation: firstly, she mistakenly thinks that the man may prefer to be with the other woman than with her and, secondly, that she is not as physically attractive as the other woman. Men are attracted visually to curves, leg lengths, and shapes. *Any* woman with the right shape and proportions will catch his attention.

It doesn't mean that the man immediately wants to race the other woman off to bed, but it is a reminder to him that he is masculine and his evolutionary role is to look for opportunities to increase the size of the tribe. After all, he doesn't even know the other woman and could not realistically be thinking about a long-term relationship with her. This same principle applies to a man looking at the centrefold in a men's magazine. When he looks at the naked woman, he doesn't wonder if she has a nice personality or can cook. He looks at her physical equipment – that's all. For him it's not much different to admiring a leg of ham hanging in a shop window. We are not making excuses for the rude, blatant ogling that some men do; we're simply explaining that if a man gets caught ogling, it doesn't mean he doesn't love his partner – it's his biology at work. In fact, studies show that women ogle more than men. Being equipped with better peripheral vision, women rarely get caught.

Women need to understand that a man is biologically compelled to look at certain female shapes and curves, and that they shouldn't feel threatened by it. An easy way for a woman to take the pressure off a man is for her to notice the other woman first and make the first comment. A man also needs to understand that no woman appreciates inappropriate ogling.

What Women Actually Look For

1. Personality

2. Humour

3. Sensitivity

4. Brains

5. Good body

What Men Think Women Look For

1. Personality

2. Good body

3. Humour

4. Sensitivity

5. Good looks

Men have a good handle on what women look for.

What Women Think Men Look For

1. Good looks

2. Good body

3. Breasts

4. Bum

5. Personality

What Men Actually Look For

1. Personality

2. Good looks

3. Brains

4. Humour

5. Good body

**Women don't really understand
what men really want.**

Women's Turn-Ons

1. Romance

2. Commitment

3. Communication

4. Intimacy

5. Non-sexual touching

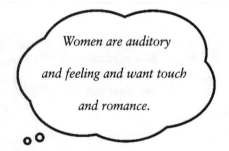

Women are auditory and feeling and want touch and romance.

Men's Turn-Ons

1. Pornography

2. Female nudity

3. Sexual variety

4. Lingerie

5. Her availability

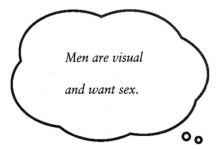

Men are visual and want sex.

How to Satisfy a Woman Every Time

Caress, praise, pamper, relish, savour, massage, fix things, empathise, serenade, compliment, support, feed, soothe, tantalise, humour, placate, stimulate, stroke, console, hug, ignore fat bits, cuddle, excite, pacify, protect, phone, anticipate, smooch, nuzzle, forgive, accessorise, entertain, charm, carry for, oblige, fascinate, attend to, trust, defend, clothe, brag about, sanctify, acknowledge, spoil, embrace, die for, dream of, tease, gratify, squeeze, indulge, idolise, worship.

How to Satisfy a Man Every Time

Arrive naked.

What women want from sex

Before sex, a woman needs to feel the build-up of tension over a longer period of time with her prerequisite of lots of attention and talk. He wants to empty; she wants to fill up. Understanding this difference makes men more caring lovers. Most women need at least 30 minutes of foreplay before they are ready for sex. Men need at least 30 seconds, and most consider driving back to her place as foreplay.

After sex, a woman is high on hormones and is ready to take on the world. She wants to touch, cuddle and talk. A man, however, if he hasn't already fallen asleep, sometimes withdraws by getting up and 'doing something' such as making coffee. A man needs to feel in control of himself at all times and, during orgasm, he temporarily loses control. Getting up and doing something allows him to regain that control.

What men want from sex

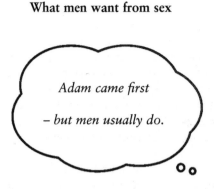

Adam came first

– but men usually do.

Men want the release of built-up tension by orgasm.

Men use sex to express physically what they can't express emotionally. If a man has a problem such as how he'll find a new job, pay the overdraft or resolve a dispute, he's likely to use sex to relieve the intensity of his emotions. There are few problems a man can have that great sex won't fix.

Tests show that a man who has a pent-up need for sex has difficulty hearing, thinking, driving or operating heavy machinery. He also suffers a form of time-distortion where 3 minutes feels like 15. If a woman wants an intelligent decision from a man she's better off discussing it after sex, when his brain is clear.

Sex Talk: Women

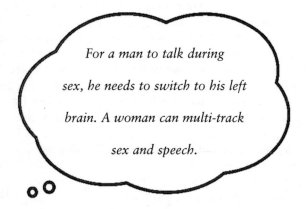

For a man to talk during sex, he needs to switch to his left brain. A woman can multi-track sex and speech.

For a woman, talk is a crucial part of foreplay because words are all-important to her. A man needs to practise lots of love talk during foreplay to fulfil a woman's needs. A woman, however, needs to stop talking during sex, and just use vocal sounds to keep a man interested – lots of 'oooh's and 'aaahs' give a man the positive feedback he needs to achieve fulfilment. If a woman talks during sex, a man feels obliged to respond and the moment can be lost.

Sex Talk: Men

Most men can only do one thing at a time. When a man has an erection he finds it difficult to speak, hear or drive, and this is why men rarely talk much during sex. Men love to hear women talk 'dirty' about what she can and will do for him – but only *before* sex, not during. A man may experience a loss of direction (and erection) when a woman talks to him during sex. During sex, a man uses his right brain, and brain scans show that he's so intent on what he is doing, he's virtually deaf.

One day God came to Adam and said, 'I've got some good news and some bad news.'

'Well, give me the good news first.'

'I've got two new organs for you. One is called a brain. It will allow you to be very intelligent, create new things, and have wonderful conversations with Eve. The other organ I have for you is called a penis. It will allow you to reproduce your new intelligent life form and populate this planet.'

Adam, very excited, exclaimed, 'These are great gifts you have given to me. What could possibly be bad news after such great tidings?'

'The bad news is that I only gave you enough blood to operate one of these organs at a time.'

Women think that computers should be referred to in the masculine gender because:

1. In order to get their attention, you have to turn them on.

2. They have a lot of data, but are still clueless.

3. They are supposed to help you solve problems, but half the time they are the problem.

4. As soon as you commit to one, you realise that, if you had waited a little longer you could have had a better model.

Men think that computers should be referred to in the feminine gender because:

1. No one but God understands their internal logic.

2. The native language they use to communicate with other computers is incomprehensible to everyone else.

3. Even your smallest mistakes are stored in long-term memory for retrieval.

4. As soon as you make a commitment to one, you find yourself spending half your salary on accessories for it.

Why Men Can Only Do One Thing at a Time...

Love, romance, marriage

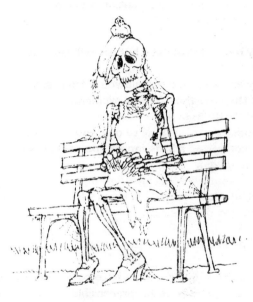

Waiting for Mr Right

... & Women Never Stop Talking

Monogamy

For a woman, marriage is a declaration to the world that a man regards her as 'special' and intends to have a monogamous relationship with her. This feeling of being 'special' has a dramatic effect on the chemical action in a woman's brain which is evidenced by research showing that a woman's orgasm rate is four to five times higher in a marital bed and two to three times higher in a monogamous relationship.

Sex is the price women pay for marriage.

Marriage is the price men pay for sex.

'…I want openness, honesty, and a monogamous
relationship. I'm not into men who want to play games!'

Why Men Can Only Do One Thing at a Time...

Polygamy

The majority of men believe having the odd fling will not affect their relationship because men have little problem separating sex from love in the brain. For women, however, sex and love are intertwined. A sexual liaison with another woman can be seen as the ultimate betrayal, and good reason for finishing a relationship.

Marriage has its good side. It teaches you loyalty, forbearance, tolerance, self-restraint, and other valuable qualities you wouldn't need if you stayed single.

Getting rid of a man without hurting his masculinity is a problem. 'Get out' and 'I never want to see you again' might sound like a challenge. If you want to get rid of a man, say 'I love you ... I want to marry you ... I want to have your children.' Sometimes they leave skid marks.

I love you

Saying 'I love you' is never a problem for a woman. A woman's brain-wiring makes her world full of feelings, emotions, communication and words. A woman knows that when she feels warm, wanted and adored and is in the attachment stage, she's probably in love. Women recognise when love does not exist and that's why most relationships are ended by women.

Women recognise when love doesn't exist.

That's why they're much more proactive

in finishing relationships.

Why men can't say the 'L' word

A man is not exactly sure what love is and he's likely to confuse lust and infatuation with love. All he knows is that he can't keep his hands off her so ... maybe that's love? His brain is blinded by testosterone, he has a constant erection and he can't think straight. It's often not until years after a relationship begins that a man recognises he was in love, but he does it in retrospect.

Many men are commitment-phobes. They are scared that saying the 'L' word commits them for the rest of their lives and spells the end of any chance of being invited to bathe with naked supermodels in jacuzzis. When a man eventually crosses the line by saying it, he then wants to tell everyone, everywhere. Most men, however, do not notice the increase in a woman's orgasm rate after he has said the 'L' word.

And finally ...

Relationships between men and women work despite overwhelming sex differences. Much of the credit here goes to women because they have the necessary skills to manage relationships and family. They're equipped with the ability to sense the motives and meanings behind speech and behaviour, and can therefore predict outcomes or take action early to avert problems. This factor alone would make the world a much safer place if every nation's leader was a woman. Men are equipped to hunt and chase lunch, find their way home, fire-gaze and procreate – that's it. They need to learn new ways for modern survival just like women do.

Relationships become rocky when men and women fail to acknowledge they are biologically different and when each expects the other to live up to their expectations. Much of the stress we experience in relationships comes from the false belief that men and women are now the same and have the same priorities, drives and desires.

For the first time in human history we are raising and educating boys and girls in identical ways, teaching them that they are the same and that each is as capable as the other. Then, as adults, they get married and wake up one morning to find they are different to each other in every way, shape and form. It's little wonder that young people's relationships and marriages are in such disastrous shape. Any concept that insists on sexual uniformity is fraught with danger because it demands the same behaviour from both men and women, who have very different brain circuitry. Sometimes it's hard to understand why Nature would plan such apparent incompatibility between the sexes, but it only looks that way because our biology is so at odds with our current environment.

The good news is that when you understand the origins of these differences, you not only find it easier to live with them, you can manage, appreciate, and end up cherishing them too.

Men want power, achievement and sex. Women want relationships, stability and love. To feel upset about this is as useful as abusing the sky for raining. Accepting that it rains allows you to cope with the weather by carrying an umbrella or raincoat, so it is no longer a problem. In the same way, anticipating the difficulties or conflicts that might arise in relationships as a result of our differences enables you to anticipate and defuse them as they occur.

Consistent and solid evidence is coming from scientists everywhere showing that biochemicals in the womb direct the structure of our brains, in turn dictating our preferences. But most of us don't need millions of dollars worth of brain-scanning equipment to know that men don't listen and women can't read maps; the equipment just explains what is often self-evident.

It's amazing that here, in the 21st century, we still don't teach an understanding of male and female relationships in our schools. We prefer to study rats running around mazes or to look at how a monkey will do backflips when conditioned by the reward of bananas. Science is a slow, lumbering discipline and takes years to feed its results into the education system.

So it's therefore up to you, the reader, to educate yourself. For only then can you hope to have relationships as happy and as fulfilling as both men and women deserve.

Why not use Allan Pease as guest speaker for your next conference or seminar?

Pease International (Australia) Pty Ltd
Pease International (UK) Ltd

P.O. Box 1260
Buderim 4556
Queensland
AUSTRALIA
Tel: ++61 (0) 5445 5600
Fax: ++61 (0) 5445 5688
email: info@peaseinternational.com
website: www.peaseinternational.com

3 Umberside Hall
Tamworth in Arden
West Midlands B94 5DF
UNITED KINGDOM
Tel: ++44 (0)1564 741888
Fax: ++44 (0)1564 741800

Also by Allan Pease:

Video Programs
  Body Language Series
  Silent Signals
  How to Make Appointments by Telephone
  The Interview
  Why Men Don't Listen and Women Can't Read Maps

Audio Cassette Programs
  Winning Moves
  The Four Personality Styles
  How to Make Appointments by Telephone
  How to Develop a Powerful Memory

Books
  Body Language
  Memory Language
  Talk Language
  Write Language
  Questions are the Answers
  Why Men Don't Listen and Women Can't Read Maps - Audio Cassette
  Why Men Cry and Women Lie

Please send for a catalogue of sales and management programs and other material by Allan Pease.